Among Those Present

A play in one act

By Aubrey Feist

WWW.SAMUELFRENCH.CO.UK
WWW.SAMUELFRENCH.COM

Copyright © 1951 Aubrey Feist
Reprinted 1953, 1959, 1964
All Rights Reserved

AMONG THOSE PRESENT is fully protected under the copyright laws of the British Commonwealth, including Canada, the United States of America, and all other countries of the Copyright Union. All rights, including professional and amateur stage productions, recitation, lecturing, public reading, motion picture, radio broadcasting, television and the rights of translation into foreign languages are strictly reserved.

ISBN 978-0-573-12007-7

www.samuelfrench.co.uk
www.samuelfrench.com

FOR AMATEUR PRODUCTION ENQUIRIES

UNITED KINGDOM AND WORLD EXCLUDING NORTH AMERICA

plays@SamuelFrench-London.co.uk

020 7255 4302/01

Each title is subject to availability from Samuel French,

depending upon country of performance.

CAUTION: Professional and amateur producers are hereby warned that AMONG THOSE PRESENT is subject to a licensing fee. Publication of this play does not imply availability for performance. Both amateurs and professionals considering a production are strongly advised to apply to the appropriate agent before starting rehearsals, advertising, or booking a theatre. A licensing fee must be paid whether the title is presented for charity or gain and whether or not admission is charged.

The professional rights in this play are controlled by Samuel French Ltd, 52 Fitzroy Street, London, W1T 5JR

No one shall make any changes in this title for the purpose of production. No part of this book may be reproduced, stored in a retrieval system, or transmitted in any form, by any means, now known or yet to be invented, including mechanical, electronic, photocopying, recording, videotaping, or otherwise, without the prior written permission of the publisher. No one shall upload this title, or part of this title, to any social media websites.

The right of Aubrey Feist to be identified as author of this work has been asserted in accordance with Section 77 of the Copyright, Designs and Patents Act 1988.

Among Those Present was televised on the 23rd November, 1948, with the following cast:

ALAN KIRBY	John Benson
CAROL PERRO	Moyra Sheldon
MRS PERRO	Margaret Boyd
GEORGE BLAKE	Campbell Singer
ERICA BLAKE	Jean Edward
PETER LYNWOOD	Ian Lubbock
THE MAID	Jean Thorburn

Production by
KEVIN SHELDON

INTRODUCTION

'AMONG THOSE PRESENT' is a little essay in the macabre, and the Producer's most important task is to see that his players behave naturally. Should he wish the audience to believe that these strange things happened, the Perros and their friends must first be accepted as real people. Tension should gradually mount from Peter Lynwood's entrance until his exit; then it relaxes a little, rising again when Carol says: 'No, not very,' and increasing until the end.

On no account should the part of George be 'guyed'. He is an army type with a big moustache; but, although we may smile at his little mannerisms, he is *not* a figure of fun, and his speech to the empty arm-chair strikes the first weird note. While he is speaking these lines, the laughter of the other characters should die away, so that he finishes in an uncomfortable silence.

The most important person in the play is, of course, Colonel Lynwood, and, although he never appears, everything possible should be done to suggest that he really is 'among those present'. Responsibility for the success of this illusion rests with the actors, who must use their imaginations and try to *see* the old gentleman. But the Producer can help them. The Colonel's arm-chair should be isolated, and, once the main light has been turned off, the standard lamp should make this chair an island of light in the shadows.

The cheroot-smoke 'business' at the end of the play can be worked by means of a rubber tube from the wings to the chair, where the end is hidden among cushions at the height of the Colonel's head. Rugs on the floor will hide the tube, down which tobacco-smoke can be blown. It requires very careful timing and plenty of rehearsal.

AUBREY FEIST.

CHARACTERS

ALAN KIRBY

CAROL PERRO

MRS. PERRO

GEORGE BLAKE

ERICA BLAKE

PETER LYNWOOD

WILSON, *the maid*

SCENE: *The lounge of Mrs. Perro's house in the country*

TIME: *A winter evening*

AMONG THOSE PRESENT

Mrs. Perro's lounge is a charming room, attractively furnished. The door leading to the hall is C, *and a bright fire is burning down* R. *There is a settee* RC, *and, upstage, a bridge table and a table for drinks. The most important piece of furniture, however, is a large arm-chair down* L, *with a small table beside it. Near this arm-chair is a lighted standard lamp.*

When the Curtain rises, CAROL PERRO *is alone in the room. She is sitting on the settee, gazing thoughtfully into the fire.* CAROL *is an attractive girl of about twenty—dark, imaginative and intense.*

The door opens and ALAN KIRBY *enters. He is a few years older than* CAROL, *but far more light-hearted and easy-going: just a pleasant, athletic type of young man. It becomes clear at once that, although he and* CAROL *are trying to behave normally, they are finding it very difficult to suppress intense emotion. The first few lines of dialogue should be delivered tensely—almost jerkily.*

ALAN. Hullo, Carol!

CAROL (*in a whisper*). Alan! (*She rises and goes to meet him,* C.) You're early.

ALAN. I know. I wanted to speak to you alone.

CAROL. But why? I don't understand. I . . .

(*It is too much for them. They can resist no longer, and suddenly they are in each other's arms. Their embrace is close and passionate; then, after tightening her arms round* ALAN *for a moment,* CAROL *wrenches herself free.*)

ALAN (*in a whisper*). Carol! Oh, my dear!

CAROL (*breathlessly*). No, darling. Not again. (*Moves to top* L. *corner of settee.*) We shouldn't have done that. Suppose we'd been seen.

ALAN. But who's to see us? The others haven't come yet.

CAROL. There's Mother.

ALAN (*moving down L to chair*). Wilson told me she was changing.

CAROL. . . . Wilson herself then.

ALAN. Hmm, yes. I suppose she might butt in. (WILSON *enters with cocktail shaker and glasses on tray. Stands up* C.) She has butted in—haven't you, Wilson?

WILSON (*smiling*). I beg your pardon, sir? (*Puts tray on 'drinks' table.*)

ALAN. . . . And at exactly the right moment. I'm dying for a drink.

WILSON. Will there be anything else, Miss Carol?

CAROL (*crossing to settee and sitting*). No, that's all, thank you, Wilson.

WILSON. Thank you, miss.

(WILSON *goes out.* ALAN *pours out a cocktail, then hesitates.*)

ALAN. Will you have one?

CAROL. No, thank you. Not now, Alan.

ALAN. Oh—right! (*Comes to* R *end of 'drinks' table. Stands facing* CAROL.)

(*There is a strained silence. He sips his drink.*)

CAROL (*quietly*). I shouldn't have let you kiss me like that. It was partly my fault. I'm sorry.

ALAN (*firmly*). I'm not.

CAROL. You forget I'm engaged.

ALAN. Oh, no, I don't. From that point of view, I suppose I'm sorry too, but . . . Well, we just couldn't help it, could we?

CAROL. No. (*Another slight pause. He finishes his cocktail, returns glass to table and comes down* C.) You've never cared much for Peter, have you?

ALAN. Oh, I don't know. He's quite a good type, but rather too highly-strung and temperamental for my taste. He has always struck me as being—well, just a trifle unbalanced—the sort of fellow who, if he were provoked, might lose his head and do anything. But there . . . I suppose I'm prejudiced. Everybody else likes him enormously.

CAROL. He's a dear.

ALAN. That's all very well. But you're not really in love with him, are you?

CAROL. I've never been really in love with him, Alan. It's taken me over a year to find out . . .

ALAN. . . . And it's taken me nearly as long to make you admit it.

CAROL. Is that why you came early to-night? To make me admit it?

ALAN. Yes.

CAROL. That was pretty rotten of you, wasn't it?

ALAN (*thoughtfully*). I'm not sure. I couldn't bear to see you throwing yourself away, that's all. I guessed some time ago that your engagement to Peter was a mistake, and honestly I'd have tried to open your eyes if I'd found you cared for somebody else. So why shouldn't I do the same for myself?

CAROL (*slowly*). I don't know.

ALAN. It may be despicable to steal another man's girl, but it's not nearly so despicable as to stand by and let that girl ruin her life.

CAROL. I'm afraid that can't be helped now, my dear. It's too late.

ALAN (*crossing to settee and sitting beside her*). Why, what do you mean? You love me, so . . .

CAROL. I mean I can't possibly break off my engagement. No,

it's no good, Alan. Peter has always been so decent to me. Besides, you're in a good job and he's still comparatively poor. He may be clever; but the little essays and poems he writes don't sell, and probably never will. He'd think . . .

ALAN. I understand. You're too honest to throw him over and marry a man with more money. (*He laughs.*) I shouldn't let that worry you, darling. He'll be disgustingly rich when his uncle dies.

CAROL. But that may not be for years. There's plenty of life in old Colonel Lynwood yet, bless his heart!

ALAN. I'm glad to hear it. I rather wondered. . . . Peter's looked so worried lately.

CAROL. He *is* worried.

ALAN. About the Colonel?

CAROL. No, about himself. I've known for some time. (*She hesitates.*) Alan—he's in a terrible mess.

ALAN. What sort of mess?

CAROL. Oh, just—debts. And I'm afraid he's been speculating rather wildly. He always was a fool about money.

ALAN. Really! I didn't know.

CAROL. He's been up to see his bankers to-day, and he's coming along presently to let me know the result. He told me last night that our wedding may have to be postponed.

ALAN (*his arm along back of settee, leaning towards her slightly*). You're quite sure it couldn't be postponed—indefinitely?

CAROL (*gazing into fire*). Quite sure, Alan! (*Swiftly turns to* ALAN). Oh, don't you see? I can't let him down. He needs me more than ever now.

(*Start fading up* CAR)

ALAN. Yes, of course I see. (*Withdrawing slightly.*) Forget it, Carol. But you mean so very much to me. I couldn't let you go without—without. . . . (*A slight pause, then he forces a laugh.*) Oh, well. . . . Which shall it be, darling? Drink or women? Or shall I go and shoot tigers, like old Colonel Lynwood? They say *he* was crossed in love once. . . . By the way, I believe I'm supposed to be a sort of stand-in for him to-night. He's ill, isn't he? I hope it's not serious.

(MRS. PERRO, *a well-groomed woman of about forty-five, enters quietly. The others do not hear her. She stands just inside the door, watching them, with a smile.*)

CAROL. No, it's only a touch of gout, but enough to keep him at home. He rang up Mother this afternoon to apologise and . .

MRS. PERRO (*smiling and coming down* LC). *Who* rang up Mother this afternoon?

ALAN (*rising and going to meet her*). Good evening, Mrs. Perro! We were talking about Peter's uncle.

MRS. PERRO. Yes, poor old, chap! He has what he calls one of his twinges. And I was so looking forward to seeing him.

CAROL. So was I.

(*Car stops.*)

MRS. PERRO. It was terribly sweet of you to take his place, Alan, but I knew how disappointed Erica would have been if we hadn't been able to make up a four. Peter's coming round later, but both he and Carol loathe cards. I do hope you didn't mind my asking you at the last minute.

ALAN. Why, of course not, Mrs. Perro. Surely we know each other well enough for that. I'm ready for bridge at any time, and my one regret is that Peter's uncle won't be able to join us. It's always good to hear that Lieutenant-Colonel Rookby Lynwood, V.C., D.S.O., etc., etc., is to be among those present. What a 'character' he is!

CAROL (*smiling*). It's sheer personality. Even at his age, he dominates any company he's in, doesn't he?

ALAN. Yes. I can see him now, sitting in that chair over there (*points to arm-chair*) smoking one of those villainous, Burma cheroots of his and—holding the floor, so to speak.

MRS. PERRO (*laughing, crosses to settee, sits L end*). Of course. He *always* sits in that chair, and he *invariably* envelops himself in a sort of private smokescreen. Dear old man!

CAROL. When he's in form, he's marvellous.

MRS. PERRO. Ah, but he has to be watched. Some of his stories of the Boer War are quite definitely ' barrack room '. I remember the Vicar was horrified once when the Colonel told him how they used to . . . (*Door bell rings.*) That'll be the Blakes.

ALAN. . . . Or Peter?

CAROL. Peter won't be here yet. He arranged to call for his uncle and bring him along in his car.

ALAN. But doesn't he know the Colonel's not coming?

MRS. PERRO. No. He told us last night that he was going up to Town first thing this morning, so it was no good 'phoning him.

(*Carol and Alan exchange glances.*)

ALAN. Yes, I believe Carol mentioned it.

MRS. PERRO. Peter's not seemed quite himself lately. He's so highly-strung, so quick-tempered and nervous. I can't make out what's the matter with him.

ALAN (*lightly*). Oh, it's just the artistic temperament, I expect. That's the trouble with most of these young authors.

MRS. PERRO. There are times when I wonder whether poor Peter isn't a trifle—well, neurotic. His behaviour in public is perfectly normal; but occasionally, when he thinks no one is looking at him, I've noticed a queer, strained expression on his face. (*She turns to her daughter.*) He's not in any trouble, is he?

CAROL (*confused*). Well, I—I . . .

ALAN (*quickly, trying to cover her*). I expect he's been overdoing it. He works terribly hard.

MRS. PERRO. Perhaps he's worried about Colonel Lynwood. (ALAN *turns away* L, *frowning. Stands by arm-chair.*) The old man must be rather a trial. He's getting very frail nowadays, do you thinking he'll do as he's told? Not he! He told me on the 'phone that he had an important letter to write this evening—to his solicitors, I believe he said. He insisted that he was going out to post it himself too—gout and all.

ALAN. But why?

MRS. PERRO. Simply to save his old housekeeper a short walk in the rain.

CAROL. I think that was rather sweet of him.

(*Voices are heard outside.* WILSON *opens the door.*)

MRS. PERRO (*firmly*). He should be sent straight to bed.

WILSON. Mr. and Mrs. Blake.

(*Enter* ERICA *and* GEORGE BLAKE. *Erica is a woman of about thirty-five, extremely smart and sophisticated.* GEORGE *is a simple soul, broad and well-built, with a ruddy complexion and military moustache. He has a bluff, hearty manner and would be the life-and-soul of a children's party.*)

ERICA		Good evening, Mrs. Perro! It's lovely to see you again. Hullo, Carol, darling.
MRS. PERRO (*rising and shaking hands*).	Together	Good evening, Erica dear! I'm so glad you've come. Good evening, George!
GEORGE (*joins* CAROL C).		Hullo, everybody! Evening, Mrs. Perro!
CAROL (*rising to* C).		Hullo, Erica! Hullo, George!
ALAN (*by chair*).		Good evening! Foul night, isn't it?

MRS. PERRO. Come and sit by the fire. You must be cold. (*Passing* ERICA *to* R, *sits* L *end of settee.*)

ERICA. My dear, I'm simply freezing. (*Sitting* R *end of settee*).

CAROL (c). Cocktails?

ERICA. Thank you.

CAROL. Alan, will you do the dispensing, please?

ALAN. Certainly.

CAROL. How about you, George? Cocktails? Sherry? Whisky?

GEORGE. Mmm! Well—er . . .

ALAN (*pouring out* ERICA'S *drink*). You've not turned T.T. by any chance?

GEORGE (*with a broad grin*). Heaven forbid! But I was born and bred a beer man. What I'd really like would be a large stoup of ale.

ERICA. George!

GEORGE (*calmly*). . . . In a can!

MRS. PERRO (*laughing*). Why, of course. (*Slight pause. She rises, rings the bell and returns to her seat.*)

ERICA (*laughing*). Please don't pander to him, Mrs. Perro. He disgraces me every time I bring him out. I'm afraid I married a man with low tastes.

GEORGE. Low tastes my foot!

ERICA. . . . A ruffian who has hardly shaken hands with his hostess before he howls loudly for ale. To think that I should have lived to see a bottle of beer on a bridge table!

GEORGE. Seems to me it'd be the one thing that would make a bridge table worth looking at.

(WILSON *enters.*)

WILSON. You rang, madam?

MRS. PERRO. Yes, Wilson. Please bring Mr. Blake a tankard of ale.

WILSON (*smiling*). Certainly, madam. (*Exit.*)

ALAN (*as he hands two drinks to* GEORGE *then one to* CAROL, *then sits on* R *arm of chair*). Not very keen on cards, are you, old man?

GEORGE. Well, no. Not particularly. (*Hands one drink to* MRS. PERRO *and one to* ERICA.) Golf's more in my line. But when one is married to a bridge fiend. . . .

ERICA (*smiling sweetly*). . . . One learns what is good for one, doesn't one—darling!

GEORGE (*in a mock 'hen-pecked' voice*). Yes, dear. (*He is* C, *on* R *of* CAROL.)

(*Laughter.*)

ERICA (*smiling*). Poor lamb!

GEORGE (*with good-humoured persistence*). I liked the sort of parties we used to have before the War. You know—when we played 'Murder' and 'Postman's Knock'. (*Chuckles.*) I had the devil of a time!

ERICA (*sighing*). My dear, you were completely licentious. I remember you at your worst. (*To the others.*) But now that he has sown his wild oats and they've—er—withered or—or whatever wild oats do, I'm afraid there are ominous signs of the approach of second childhood.

CAROL (*laughing*). What do you mean?

ERICA. His one idea of fun-and-games nowadays is to indulge in childish pranks. He adores practical jokes—apple-pie beds and exploding cigarettes. (*She sighs again.*) My life's a misery.

GEORGE. Nonsense! (*Crosses to fire, stands with his back to it.*) Don't you believe her. I'm not really as bad as that. (*Eagerly.*) But talking of practical jokes, I remember one we put over on our chaplain during the war. It was while I was at Dortmund. The Adjutant, a chap named Pottinger, had gone home on leave, and . . . (*The door opens.*) . . . And talking of the Army, this must be old Lynwood.

(ERICA *motions him to be quiet. Enter* WILSON *with a large silver tankard of ale on a salver. She brings it down* R *to* GEORGE.)

CAROL. No, I'm afraid Colonel Lynwood can't come to-night. Peter is calling for him, but the poor old thing has a bad attack of gout and . . .

ALAN (*smiling*). . . . And that's why *I'm* here.

GEORGE. Oh, bad show! (*Hastily.*) It's hard luck on the Colonel I mean.

WILSON. Your beer, sir. (*Offers tankard on salver to* GEORGE.)

GEORGE. Thanks, Wilson! You've saved my life. (*Raises tankard.*) Cheery-bung, troops!

ERICA (*pretending to be horrified*). Cheery-bung! I ask you!
(*Exit* WILSON.)

CAROL (*to* GEORGE). You were saying. . . . (*Sits on stool.*)

GEORGE. Oh, yes. I was telling you about that trick we played. It was absolutely wizard! The poor old padre had just returned from leave, so naturally he didn't know that Pottinger was away, and we nearly scared the life out of him by pretending the fellow was there all the time.
(*Puzzled smiles.*)

MRS. PERRO. What do you mean?

ALAN (*crossing to just above and* L *of* CAROL). Pretending *who* was there?

(*The positions are now:* GEORGE—*back to fire.* ERICA—R *end of settee.* MRS. PERRO—L *end of settee.* CAROL—*on stool, facing* GEORGE. ALAN—*standing above* CAROL *and to her* L.)

GEORGE. Why, Captain Pottinger, our Adjutant.

MRS. PERRO. I'm afraid I—still—don't—quite—see . . .

ALAN (*laughing*). It's certainly too deep for *me*.

GEORGE (*patiently*). But, my dear Alan, it's quite simple. We were all in it, you understand, and we played up for all we were worth. As I've just said, we talked and behaved as if the absent Pottinger were there in the Mess with us. Asked his advice, answered imaginary questions, chaffed him, laughed at his jokes, and so on. It went on for hours.

ERICA (*coolly*). Why?

GEORGE (*not in the least abashed*). Eh? Oh, it was just our idea of a merry little jest, sweetheart mine.

CAROL. And how did it end?

GEORGE. Oh, we had to blow the gaff. The poor old padre thought he was going mad. It must have been pretty foul to hear everyone talking to a man who wasn't there.

CAROL (*smiling*). What a shame!

GEORGE. You should have seen his face! Whiter than his own Sunday surplice!

ALAN. That's all very well. But what sort of man was this chaplain of yours?

GEORGE. Oh, quite a good type. But he'd been preaching at me rather too much, so . . .

ALAN. Quite! What I really meant was—was he particularly gullible?

GEORGE. Good heavens, no! Why?

ALAN. Then I'm surprised the trick worked, that's all.

GEORGE. My dear old boy, it'll always work if you keep it up long enough and if everybody plays the game. It's a question of—of mass suggestion. It might be necessary—I won't say to lie, but to—er—prevaricate a little—and of course one laugh would ruin everything.

CAROL. (*thoughtfully*). Yes, I believe it *would* work. In the end, if it were well done, you'd almost *see* the person. It would be most uncanny.

ERICA (*firmly*). Well, I'm not convinced. You mustn't forget that you're Cornish—a primitive, superstitious Celt. We common-or-garden Anglo-Saxons would prefer to believe the evidence of our own eyes and ears.

GEORGE. Oh, I'm not so sure. Would *you*? Well, perhaps you would. You're so—er—strong-minded, star of my soul! But I think most people would be taken in. Suppose, for example, when Peter Lynwood arrived to-night, we all behaved as if his uncle had turned up after all. I believe, after a time he'd be ready to swear that the Colonel was sitting over there in his usual chair, puffing away at a big cigar and . . .

MRS. PERRO. It's certainly an amusing idea.

CAROL. It *could* be rather horrible.

ERICA. Well, *I* think it's too childish for words. Peter may be a poet and a dreamer, but he's not a damn fool. He'd see through our play-acting in a minute and merely conclude that we'd all gone crackers.

GEORGE (*shaking his head*). Oh, no, he wouldn't, my dear. I know. I've seen it done. I'm ready to bet anything you like . . .

ERICA. All right! I'll take you.

GEORGE. Eh?

ALAN (*laughing*). You can't get out of it now, George. You've ' had ' it!

ERICA (*pleasantly, looking round her*). An idea like this could only have been hatched in the brain of a congenital idiot; but, if you people are willing, it might be worth while putting it to the test. (*Murmurs of assent. She turns to* GEORGE.) Now listen! This is a bet. If you lose, you'll trot along to bridge parties for the next six months without a murmur.

(GEORGE *groans.*)

GEORGE. Very well. And if I win?

ERICA (*laughing*). Then I'll—I'll go pub-crawling or play 'Ring-a-ring-a-roses'. Anything you like. (*Turns to the others.*) Trust George to start something like this. I came here to play bridge.

ALAN. But it won't take long, and it'll be rather fun. What do you say, Mrs. Perro?

MRS. PERRO. Oh, it'll be all right, I suppose. But we mustn't carry the joke too far.

ERICA. Don't worry. Peter will see to that. I've a great respect for Peter's intelligence.

CAROL (*crossing to door*). I'll go and tell Wilson. (ALAN *reaches door first and opens it for her. After* CAROL'S *exit, he remains by door.*) She must be in this too, otherwise she might give the game away. Later on, she can come in and speak to the imaginary Colonel. (*Exit.*)

(*Start fading up car.*)

GEORGE. I say! That's a bright idea.

ALAN. Yes, it'll shake Peter to his foundations. Who on earth would suspect Wilson? (*He laughs.*) Do you know, this will be rather like H. G. Wells's 'Invisible Man'.

GEORGE. Exactly! (*He holds up his hand.*) Quiet, everybody, please! Let's get this straight. (*He waits for silence, enjoying himself immensely.*) Now we don't do anything funny or odd, but just carry on as if Colonel Lynwood were really in the room with us. I know! Let's put the light out and leave just the standard lamp. That'll make it more creepy.

ALAN (*switching off light*). How's that? (*He goes down* R *behind settee.*)

GEORGE. Fine!

(*Car stops.*)

(*The room is now dimly lit by the red, flickering firelight. There is only one pool of radiance; and this, cast by the standard lamp, draws every eye to the big arm-chair.*)

MRS. PERRO (*entering into the spirit of the game*). Look! There's the Colonel, sitting over there in his usual chair.
(*The others laugh, but their laughter gradually dies as* GEORGE *speaks quietly.*)

GEORGE. Of course he is. Smoking a big black cheroot. I hope you can all see him. (*Pause. He crosses to the chair, speaking quite naturally and waiting politely for the old gentleman's answer.*) I'm so glad you could come after all, sir. Your nephew is late. I beg your pardon? I didn't quite catch . . . (*Laughs.*) Oh, yes, yes. Quite! I expect he is! As you say, we're only young once.

ERICA (*slowly, after a slight pause*). Yes—I see what you mean, George. This stupid trick of yours could be quite convincing.
(*Door bell rings.*)

GEORGE (*briskly*). Right! Then are we all set? (*The others nod.*) Now remember, we're all on our honour not to give the show away until poor old Peter is thoroughly rattled. If one of us laughs in the wrong place, it'll kill the whole thing stone dead.

ERICA (*half laughing, half serious*). It's really rather a mean trick to play on the boy. And it might be dangerous. (*Crosses to* GEORGE.) You never know where you are with these sensitive, artistic people.

GEORGE. Nonsense! (*Moving up to* LC.) It's quite harmless. And I don't think a ragging will do young Peter any harm. He's rather too fond of poking fun at other people. Satire, he calls it. I've more than a suspicion that we all appear in that novel he's writing.

ERICA (*frowning*). What!

GEORGE (*drily*). I know there's a horrible hearty type called George with about as much brain as a mangel-wurzle. And George has a wife . . .

ERICA. Oh! (*She turns on her heel, goes up 'drinks' table and puts down glass.*)

(*Enter* WILSON.)

WILSON. Mr. Lynwood.

MRS. PERRO (*in a hurried whisper*). He's early.

ALAN. We were just in time.

(PETER LYNWOOD *comes into the room. He is an extremely good-looking young man with thick, wavy hair and a pale, sensitive face. His voice is soft and musical.* (*Exit* WILSON.) *Greetings are exchanged. Taking out his lighter,* GEORGE *walks across to the empty arm-chair and lights the* COLONEL'S *cheroot.* PETER *gives him a surprised glance but makes no comment.*)

PETER. Good evening, everybody! (*Going towards* MRS. PERRO.) How are you, Mrs. Perro?

MRS. PERRO (*rising and shaking hands*). Very well, thank you, Peter, dear.

PETER. Where's Carol?

MRS. PERRO. She'll be here in a minute. (*Smiling.*) Well, aren't you going to say good evening to your uncle?

(PETER *stares at her.*)

(ERICA *moves down to arm-chair and leans on the back of it as if talking to the* COLONEL.)

PETER (*quietly*). My uncle? (*Pause. He does* NOT *look round.*) What do you mean?

MRS. PERRO (*with a pleasant smile*). Just what I said.

PETER (*with a puzzled frown*). But—but I don't understand. When I called at his cottage to pick him up, I was told that he couldn't come to-night, on account of his gout. He can't be very bad though. His housekeeper said he'd just gone down to the village to post a letter.

GEORGE. So he did, but he changed his mind and came on here instead—didn't you, Colonel? (*Turning away and taking empty tankard to 'drinks' table.*) Erica and I happened to see him and gave him a lift.

PETER (*utterly flabbergasted*). But—but . . .

ERICA (*laughing, as if the* COLONEL *had just said something amusing*). What's that? Oh, you wicked old man! Please stop him, Mrs. Perro.

MRS. PERRO (*shaking her finger at the empty arm-chair*). Now then, Colonel! How could you! You've actually made Erica blush.

(CAROL *comes in carrying a book.*)

CAROL (*laying the book on the small table beside the arm-chair*). That's the book we were talking about, Colonel. I think it's rather amusing. (*She listens.*) Yes, certainly. Of course you can borrow it. (*She crosses to* PETER, *who is staring at her in an almost frightened manner.*) Hullo, darling! (*She kisses him lightly, then goes up* L *and talks to* GEORGE.)

PETER (*forcing a laugh*). Is this a joke? If so, I'll buy it.

GEORGE (*raising his eyebrows*). Joke?

MRS. PERRO. What do you mean, Peter?

PETER (*half laughing, half annoyed*). But what's the idea? Talking to my uncle as if he were here—as if he . . .

ALAN. Why on earth shouldn't we talk to your uncle?

PETER (*wheeling on him*). But how can you? I mean . . . Well, is he here to talk to? Is he in this room.

ERICA (*coolly*). You'd better ask him.

PETER (*his jaw dropping*). Ask him? Ask . . .

(*His eyes slowly fix themselves on the arm-chair. Pause. Then the door opens. Enter* WILSON.)

WILSON. Colonel Lynwood is wanted on the telephone.

PETER (*almost inaudibly*). Oh, my God! Am I going mad?

GEORGE (*politely*). Allow me, sir. (*He gives the* COLONEL *his arm and slowly helps him to the door, where he hands him over to* WILSON. *The others watch in silence.* WILSON *in turn gives the old gentleman her arm, then suddenly starts coughing, looks up as if the* COLONEL *had said something—and smiles.*)

WILSON. Oh, no, sir. (*She coughs again.*) It's quite all right, sir, really! The smoke from your cigar, that's all.
(*Exit* WILSON *and the* COLONEL *very slowly.* GEORGE *closes the door. There is complete silence which lasts for a second or two after the door has closed. Then the tension is eased. Conversation flows on again quite naturally.*)

CAROL. I don't believe we've offered Peter a cocktail. Cocktail, Peter? (PETER *is down* R, *his eyes fixed on the door. He does not hear* CAROL *at first. She raises her voice.*) Peter!

PETER (*starting*). Eh? What's that? I—I beg your pardon?

MRS. PERRO. Will you have a cocktail? (*She goes to 'drinks' table, then nods to* ERICA, *who joins her.*)

PETER. Oh, yes—yes. Thanks very much!
(MRS. PERRO *is talking to the Blakes up* L. CAROL *joins them.* ALAN *pours out a cocktail and brings it down* R *to* PETER, *who is standing by himself, obviously ill at ease. He is trying not to watch the door, but from time to time he glances towards it.*)

ALAN. Well, how's the world been treating you lately?

PETER. Not too badly.

ALAN (*casually*). And how's business? Sold any essays?

PETER. Well—no; but things are looking up, and I believe my first novel's going to be a winner. (*He laughs uneasily.*) I've been rather worried about money lately, but—but that's all over now.

ALAN (*giving him a quick glance of surprise*). Really? I'm so glad. I suppose you're looking forward to getting married?

PETER. Yes.

ALAN. It's to be in April, isn't it?

PETER (*with another furtive glance towards the door*). . . . . Yes.
(CAROL *joins them.* ALAN *turns away to join the others, but hesitates at* C, *turns, and overhears* CAROL *and* PETER.)
CAROL (*in a low voice to* PETER). What sort of day have you had in Town?
PETER (*bitterly*). Terrible!
(ALAN *just hears him. He looks round again with a puzzled frown, but* PETER *is drinking his cocktail and does not notice.*)
CAROL (*in a whisper*). Oh! (*Then as* PETER *goes to the mantelpiece to put down his empty glass, she remembers the part she has promised to play and forces herself to speak brightly. She goes to* ALAN, C) Mother was just saying it was about time you began your game Alan. Will you help George down with the table? He's as pleased as Punch that he won't have to play after all.
ALAN. Yes, we can make up a four without him, can't we, now that Colonel Lynwood has turned up?
PETER (*wheeling on him savagely, but speaking in a low, suppressed voice.*) Oh, for God's sake, stop this nonsense, Kirby!
ALAN. What nonsense?
PETER. I can take a joke. It's damn funny! But if you keep it up too long it becomes boring and—and . . .
CAROL. Peter, what are you talking about? (*Crossing to* PETER, R.) Have you been drinking?
(ALAN *sits on* L *arm of settee.*)
PETER (*quite seriously. Strangely enough, he seems relieved*). Yes—that must be it. I'm drunk. I—I had one or two on the way here, but I've a good head for whisky. I never dreamed that one could get D.T's. so easily.
CAROL (*staring at him.*) D.T's.?
PETER (*unsteadily, controlling himself with an effort*). Yes! D.T's!—D.T's!—Delirium tremens! It makes you see things—and

people—that aren't really there! It makes you think you're going mad! It makes you . . .

ERICA (*coming down to just above arm-chair*). Peter! Come here! I want you. What do you think your uncle said just now?

PETER (*with a ghastly smile*). I—I haven't the faintest idea.

(*He crosses to* ERICA *and stands back to audience, his eyes on the door.* ERICA *tells her story quietly during the next few lines of dialogue between* CAROL *and* ALAN.)

CAROL (*with a worried glance at* PETER, *as she sits on settee by* ALAN.) Alan, don't you think we'd better . . .

ALAN. Ssh! (*His face is grave now as he motions her to be quiet, but she goes on in a low, angry tone——*)

CAROL. This joke has gone far enough. Peter's scared stiff.

ALAN (*grimly*). Yes—and so soon too! I'm surprised. In fact, there's something infernally queer here that I don't understand. . . . Look!

(*The door has begun to open slowly.* PETER *gives a gasp of horror; then runs to it, slams it again, and stands with his back to it, arms outstretched and palms flat against the panels.*)

PETER (*hysterically*). Don't let him in! Don't let him in! DON'T LET HIM IN! (*His voice rises to a scream; on* PETER'S *scream,* ALAN *springs up and moves down to fire;* ERICA *draws back* L, *then, all at once, something snaps in* PETER'S *overwrought brain and he realizes that it is useless to continue the struggle. He is calm now. Slowly, mechanically, he opens the door and we catch a glimpse of* WILSON *outside. There is a tense and horrified silence as he takes the* COLONEL'S *arm from* WILSON *and leads the old gentleman back towards his chair.* MRS. PERRO *and* GEORGE *move about settee.*)

GEORGE (*in a whisper*). My God! What have we done?

(GEORGE *starts to move forward,* MRS. PERRO *stops him. She glances at the others. All but* ALAN *nod. She steps quickly forward.*)

MRS. PERRO. Peter!

PETER (*speaking quite naturally as he joins her,* C). Yes?
(*There are sighs of relief. The tension slackens.*)

MRS. PERRO. Peter, I do hope you'll accept our apologies for playing this idiotic trick on you. We're all terribly sorry.

GEORGE. Hear, hear!

PETER (*with a puzzled frown*). Sorry? Why, what for?

GEORGE. For pretending that Colonel Lynwood was in the room of course.

(PETER *laughs.*)

PETER (*quietly and pleasantly*). Do you know, I thought you *were* fooling at first. Don't know what's the matter with me. It must have been that Scotch. There must be a certain stage of drunkenness that creates a—a sort of blind spot in the brain.

ERICA (*sharply moving to* PETER, C). What do you mean?

PETER (*calmly*). I couldn't see my own uncle.
(*Dead silence. Count of* 2. MRS. PERRO *draws away from him and moves back to her place behind settee.*)

GEORGE (*in a horrified whisper*). I shall never forgive myself for this.

PETER (*helping the* COLONEL *into his chair again*). There you were, sir, as large as life, and I was certain—I was quite *sure* that this chair was empty—that—that you weren't here at all. Isn't it absurd?

ERICA (*losing her nerve*). Peter—shut up! SHUT UP! Do you hear.

PETER (*mildly*). I beg your pardon, Erica?

ERICA. The joke's on us. You've had your own back.
(*The positions are now:* PETER—C. ALAN—*by fire.* CAROL— L *end of settee.* MRS. PERRO *and* GEORGE—*behind settee.* ERICA—*up* L.)

PETER (*mystified*). But I'm not joking. (*She draws back.*) I'm quite serious. Why are you all looking at me so strangely? (*To chair.*) I'm glad you *are* here, Uncle. So glad! (*In a whisper.*) It means that the other was only a dream.

(ALAN *gives a slight start.*)

GEORGE (*thoroughly frightened*). Peter, for God's sake, snap out of it! This is horrible.

PETER (*utterly bewildered*). But why? What have I said? What have I done? Have you all gone crazy—or have I? First you tell me that Uncle's here, and then you say he isn't. I thought you were right at first. Everything seemed so—so peculiar, but now . . . (*Turns to chair.*) Speak to them Uncle. Tell them to stop fooling. A joke's a joke, but there are limits and . . . (*Suspiciously.*) You're not in this too, are you? Why don't you speak? *His voice rises and there is a sob in it.*) Don't just sit there smoking and grinning at me! Take that damned cigar out of your mouth! and . . . (*Pleadingly.*) Oh, I know you were angry with me yesterday. You ordered me out of the house, didn't you, and threatened to disinherit me? But surely—surely . . .

ALAN (*quietly crossing* C. *to* PETER). Don't think me inquisitive, Peter, but what was the row about?

PETER. What do you think? Money! Money! Debts! I'm dead broke, but it isn't my fault and . . .

ALAN. But you told me just now that things were all right again.

PETER (*dully*). Did I? Well, what does it matter? They will be all right soon.

ALAN. Why?

PETER (*passing his hand over his eyes*). I don't know. I can't think clearly. I—I can't remember.

ALAN. Let's ask Colonel Lynwood, shall we?

GEORGE (*sharply*). Alan, drop it! Can't you see that the poor devil isn't responsible for what he's saying?

MRS. PERROT } *Together* { Yes, hadn't you better leave him alone, Alan.
ERICA } { I can't stand any more of this!

ALAN. Quiet! Quiet! everybody, please!

GEORGE. What the hell do you mean, ordering us about!

ALAN. I'm sorry, but I'm afraid I must insist. You see, I think I know what's happened. (*When silence is restored, he turns to* PETER, *crossing in front of him to chair.*) And now, my friend, I'm going to ask the Colonel to explain things a little more clearly. (*Bending down to chair.*) Colonel Lynwood, what did your nephew mean just now when he told me his money troubles were over? A few minutes later he contradicted himself and said he was up to his ears in debt. What's that? Exactly! So I understood. You heard he'd been playing the fool, and threatened to cut him out of your will. (*He turns to* PETER.) Correct, old man?

PETER (*dully*). Yes.

ALAN (*to the chair*). Then it's pretty clear, sir, that Peter wasn't telling me the truth when he said 'things are looking up'. If he's facing disinheritance, he's in a worse mess than ever. (*Waits as if for an answer, then laughs.*) Oh, I see. You haven't made your new will yet. Then I suppose there's still a chance that you may change your mind? I'm sure I hope so. . . . I beg your pardon? You say I'd better ask your nephew? Oh, very well. If you insist. (*Turns to* PETER.) What's the position, Peter?

PETER (*in a dull, flat voice*). The position is hopeless. He's as hard as nails. He said he was going to write to his solicitor to-night.

CAROL (*quickly*). Then that was the letter the Colonel was going out to post.

MRS. PERRO (*to* ALAN). You remember. He told me on the 'phone . . .

(PETER *slowly puts one hand into his pocket.* ALAN *is watching him closely.*)

ALAN (*appealing for silence*). Please!

ERICA. But why should we be quiet? We don't understand. Why do you go on talking to Colonel Lynwood? You know as well as we do that he isn't here.

ALAN (*quietly*). Perhaps his ghost is here, Erica.

(*A light seems to dawn on* PETER.)

PETER (*eagerly*). Yes, that's it! His ghost! Now I understand. That's why I couldn't see him at first, and why you can't see him now. (*Shrilly, pointing to chair.*) That's not a real man at all! That's not my uncle! It's only his spirit.

(*When* PETER *points to chair, all look at* PETER.)

CAROL. But Colonel Lynwood's still alive. You can't be a ghost until—until you're . . .

ALAN . . . Dead! Exactly! (*To chair.*) Now we're getting nearer the truth, aren't we, sir? It's because you're dead that you've come here to-night after all. It's because your're dead that Peter's financial difficulties have been settled. And it's because he *knew* you were dead that he was so surprised to see you sitting there. (*Sharply.*) Am I right? (*He kneels to hear the* COLONEL'S *reply.*) You hear that, Peter? Your uncle says it's a lucky thing for you that he had no time to alter his will. It's lucky for you that he died before he could post that letter.

MRS. PERRO (*in a whisper*). Before—he—could—post . . .

ALAN. Yes. Unless I'm very much mistaken, that letter is in Peter's pocket now. (PETER, *who is standing motionless, with wide, staring eyes slowly draws a letter from his pocket and tears it into small pieces.*) And now the Colonel wants Peter to tell us in his own words just what happened this evening.

(*It never occurs to* PETER *to disobey that shadowy figure in the chair. He begins to speak very slowly, but his voice gradually rises until it is vibrating with emotion.*)

PETER. I promised to call for Uncle at eight o'clock and bring him here in my car.

ALAN. I know. But did that arrangement still hold good? I mean—after your quarrel?

PETER. Oh, yes. He agreed to say nothing about it to anyone. It's no use washing your dirty linen in public. Outwardly we were still to be good friends. Good friends! My God!

ALAN (*softly*). Go on!

PETER. I've been up in London all day, trying to save something from the wreck. It was awful! The bankers told me that there was no hope at all. It meant the end of everything. I was desperate. I—I hardly knew what I was doing. You see, when I broke the news to Uncle last night he was utterly cruel and pitiless. Swore that I shouldn't inherit a penny of his. And I knew that he meant what he said. (*He sneers.*) You always were a hard man, weren't you, Uncle? In your heart you've always despised me for hating war and sport, for worshipping beauty, for being what you call ' soft '.

ALAN. It's no good going on at Colonel Lynwood. He wants you to tell us what happened.

PETER (*staring at him blankly*). Oh, yes—yes. Where was I? (*He thinks for a moment; then as it comes back to him, a look of fear and horror comes into his eyes.*) As I was driving down the dark lane, I suddenly saw the figure of a man in the glare of my headlights. It was you, Uncle. You were carrying something white in your hand—the letter to the solicitors— that damned letter which meant ruin for me, utter and irretrievable! It would have been difficult enough to avoid you at the best of times, but somehow—I simply didn't try. Something seemed to snap in my brain. In that split second—

terribly clearly—I saw the way out of all my troubles. Instead of swerving, I accelerated. I drove straight into you—over you—didn't I? I believe you screamed once. Then there was a horrible bump and . . .

GEORGE (*in a whisper*). Murder!

ALAN. Yes—murder!

(PETER *turns to* ALAN. *Although he is quite mad, confession has calmed him and soothed his tortured nerves. Once more he speaks quietly, precisely, choosing his words.*)

PETER. It must have been what they call a brainstorm. I—I just saw red. A moment later I was horrified—appalled by what I had done. (*He gives a wicked little chuckle.*) But only for a moment! When I saw that dear Uncle was really dead, I became quite calm and very cunning. Oh, yes! Very, very cunning. I cleaned the car, drove straight on, and called at the cottage as arranged.

GEORGE (*softly*). You young swine!

ERICA. Quiet, George! Let him go on.

(PETER *does not seem to hear them.*)

PETER. The housekeeper told me that poor Uncle was not feeling very well. (*With a cunning smile.*) Naturally, I asked to see him. She said he had gone out to post a letter—a most important letter to his solicitors. (*Again that insane chuckle.*) An important letter to his solicitors! Wasn't it clever of me to have guessed?

(PETER *is smiling and muttering to himself.* ALAN *turns to the others.*)

ALAN. Perhaps you see now why I insisted on going through with this horrible farce!

MRS. PERRO. Yes. But how did you come to suspect . . .

GEORGE. Never mind that now, Mrs. Perro. We must ring the police at once.

ERICA. I will. (*Exit.*)

MRS. PERRO (*with a shudder*). Hadn't we better take that poor boy away from—— (*She points to the empty chair*) ——him?

GEORGE. Yes, perhaps we had better.

MRS. PERRO (*kindly, taking* PETER'S *arm*). Come along, Peter. George and I are going into the dining-room. We've something to show you. It's—it's a surprise.

PETER (*with almost childish enthusiasm*). Have you? How marvellous I hope it's something nice. (MRS. PERRO *and* GEORGE *start to lead him out of the room. At the door, he stops suddenly, shakes himself free and faces the chair.*) I want Uncle to go with me.

MRS. PERRO (*soothing him*). Uncle will join us later, my dear.

PETER (*peevishly*). But why not now? Oh, very well. (*Turns to chair.*) Don't be long, Uncle. There are lots of things I want to tell you. Lovely things about my work. I'm getting on with my novel, and I began a new poem yesterday. It's really rather clever. You've always jeered at my poems, but I'm sure that when you've heard this one . . . It's called ' To a skylark '. Some people say Shelley wrote it, but don't you believe them. It's my masterpiece. At least I—I think it is. Shelley told me so himself, when we walked together in our dream. Listen. . . .

> ' Hail to thee, blithe spirit!
> Bird thou never wert . . .
> That from heaven or near it
> Pourest thy full heart
> In profuse strains of unpremeditated art. . . . '

(*He is still reciting the famous ode in a lifeless, sing-song voice as* MRS. PERRO *and* GEORGE *lead him away.* CAROL *and* ALAN *are alone once more in the dim, firelit room. There is a long silence.* CAROL, *who is crying, sinks down on to the settee.* ALAN *stands just behind her. He is frowning. Once he glances almost nervously at the arm-chair standing in its little island of light.*)

CAROL. He's quite mad. Poor, poor Peter! (*Slight pause.*) Alan, can't you say something?

ALAN (*bitterly*). What *can* I say? Believe me, I'm not very proud of having successfully disposed of my rival. But what else could I do? You see, I—I guessed what had happened.

CAROL. You mean about Colonel Lynwood's death? But that's absurd. How could you possibly . . .

ALAN (*coming down on her* L). There were several small things that set me thinking. To begin with, the way he contradicted himself about his money troubles. And then—well, what would *you* do if you entered a room and were asked to say ' good evening ' to somebody you hadn't seen?

CAROL. Oh, I don't know. Look round, I suppose, and then . . .

ALAN. Exactly! Of course you would. So would most people. But when your mother said: ' Aren't you going to say good evening to your uncle, Peter? ' he appeared strangely shocked and terrified—*but he never looked round*. I could tell from his manner that he *knew* the Colonel couldn't be here.

CAROL (*slowly and thoughtfully*). I see!

ALAN. Then, when we had convinced him, there was that extraordinary remark of his: ' I'm so glad you're here, Uncle. It means that the other was only a dream '.

CAROL. Yes, I noticed it at the time. It was odd, but I didn't think it meant anything.

ALAN. It meant the deuce of a lot. The other! What other? The only explanation I could think of was that Peter had seen the Colonel before, this evening, in circumstances which he preferred to forget. It was *that*—together with a display of sheer terror which went far beyond anything I had expected— that finally convinced me that there had been foul play.

(*Quietly and soberly.*) And—and somehow I guessed that Peter had killed his uncle. Queer, isn't it?

CAROL (*staring into the fire*). No, not very.

ALAN (*sharply*). What do you mean?

CAROL. Perhaps someone told you.

ALAN. Are you crazy? Who could have possibly . . .

CAROL. Colonel Lynwood! (*With a queer smile, she gets up and puts both hands on* ALAN'S *shoulders. He stands motionless.*) I never thought I was psychic; but, do you know, I've such a strange feeling—as if we had called on the Devil in jest, and then found, to our horror, that he was standing just behind us. We got more than we bargained for this evening, Alan.

ALAN. We certainly did!

CAROL (*intensely*). You can talk about Peter's guilty conscience and autosuggestion as much as you like. There was more in it than that. We called Colonel Lynwood—and I believe he came! I've been conscious of it for a long time. I could have sworn that he was in the room with us. Perhaps he *was* in the room. (*She lowers her voice.*) Perhaps he's still here!

ALAN. Steady on, Carol!

CAROL. I suppose you're laughing at me because I'm a superstitious Celt; but don't you think it's possible that, in some way, the old man *did* avenge his murder?

ALAN. No, I don't.

(CAROL *looks at him for a moment, then sighs and turns away as if she realizes that she will never make him understand.*)

CAROL. Maybe you're right. I—I don't know. (*Suddenly she clings to him.*) Alan, I'm frightened! We're not alone in this room! I know it! I can feel it!

ALAN (*gently*). Of course we're alone. (*With a shade of uneasiness*). You can't see anything?

CAROL. No, nothing at all. It's just that strange, uncanny feeling—and a faint smell like—like cigar smoke!

ALAN (*in an awed voice*). That's funny. Do you know, a moment ago, *I* thought I could smell a Burma cheroot. A Burma cheroot! Imagination, of course. Otherwise, it wouldn't make sense. It would mean . . .

CAROL (*in a whisper*). You said you smelt cigar smoke? . . . Look!
  (*Drawing back, she raises her arm and points. From the empty arm-chair a blue coil of smoke is slowly rising. It drifts away and fades into the shadows.*)

CURTAIN.

STAGE PLAN

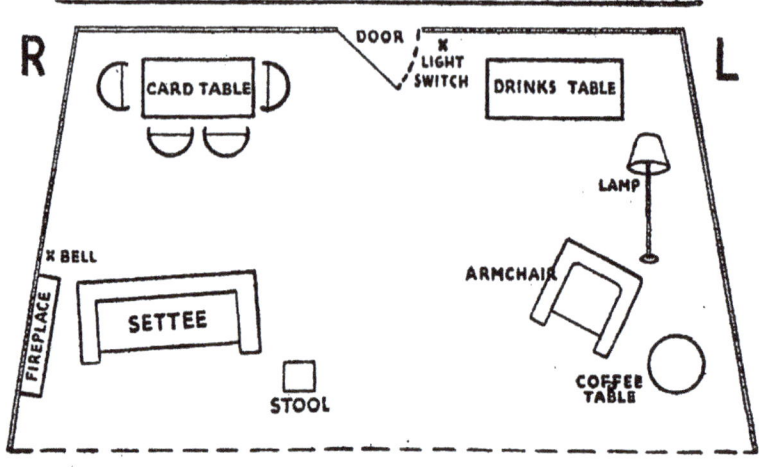

FURNITURE

Settee with cushions.
Arm-chair with cushions.
Standard lamp and shade.
Stool.
Coffee table.

Card table with four chairs round it.
'Drinks' table or cocktail cabinet.
Ornaments for fireplace.

PROPERTIES

Cocktail shaker, tray and six glasses.
Decanters, etc., on 'drinks' table.
Cigarette-box, lighter, and ash-tray on coffee table. (Cigarettes in box.)

Bell-push by fireplace.
Light-switch by door.
Silver (pint) tankard of beer on salver (WILSON).
Book (CAROL).
Lighter (GEORGE).
Letter (PETER).

EFFECTS

Door-bell.
Car.

Lighted fire.
Cigar-smoke (see Introduction).

www.ingramcontent.com/pod-product-compliance
Lightning Source LLC
Chambersburg PA
CBHW061518040426
42450CB00008B/1680